OVERHEARD

OVERHEARD

Poems

Edward Lemond

Breachhouse Books
Barachois, New Brunswick

Lemond, Edward

Overheard

ISBN:

978-0-9780510-5-1

First Paperback Edition, 2011

Second, Expanded Edition, 2012

Third, Expanded Edition, 2013

Fourth, Corrected Edition, 2016

Breachhouse Books

Chemin de la Brèche

Barachois, N.B.

E-mail: elemond@bellaliant.net

Printed in the United States of America at

www.lulu.com

For Elaine

Contents

OVERHEARD

Home From Germany

You can have the roasted Makrele and the pony ride;
I will walk down the hill to the local diner
and sit at the counter with my soggy French fries.
And you can have the garden and the wading pool
behind Herr Schnurre's house,
if I can have the field where the cows
graze on silk and alfalfa.
And you are free to roam the Bird Park
with its mighty macaws and lofty cockatoos,
if you let me stay to watch the fishermen
below on the wharf loading lobster traps.

If the sailors did come they would pick Pino's.
That is where the sun and the moon would stand still.
That is where the grass would be burned.

I have been saying this for years.
I have been standing in the window
above fire hydrants and foreign fishing vessels.
I have been leaning against the garden fence,
surrounded by pine needles and brooms,
counting bodies in the moonlight.

The Necessity Of Belief
After reading Krishnamurti

Before dawn I went down
to the beach below the house,
to the edge of the dark water.
Listening to the silence,
I learned to be silent.
Everything happening
around me was part of me.
In the distance a dog barked
and the day had begun.

Coming back, I saw pigeons
on the railing of the balcony.
The stone tower,
so close across the bay,
was flooded with light.
But long before the pigeons
were on the balcony,
on the hillside waking
was gladness.

Standing with friends
above the green bay,
I saw a girl leaning
against the boathouse,
watching us with complete
indifference, with no care
for who we were.
Her dress was dirty,
and her hair, it seemed,
had not been washed for days.
Because of her indifference,
she was like a grown-up
young woman, and when
she started to walk away,
on the path through the woods,
it was I who walked away,
who knelt in the dirt,
who picked up the stick,
who turned and threw it
into the churning water.

Deep thoughts and deep acts,
beyond anyone's understanding,
open the gates of the heart.

At a stoplight I saw the sun
in the tops of the trees,
so big and so red
it was unreal. Everything
was alive and bursting
with color, and as the sun
went down, every color
became more violent.
It was a burning, living,
exploding, dying light.
I was annihilated,
far beyond any desire.

In a house along the road
I heard voices quarrelling.
There's never enough
money, a woman cried,
for meat or eggs. Even
from far away I could hear
her voice, so clearly
it seemed to signal
the end of something.
Is there no death then?
There is a withering away,
the body grows old,
it gets worn out,
but that is inevitable.
Is that the cause of our fear?
The world of wanting,
striving, achieving
lacks all validity.
Life is here and now,
the active present,
the wind, the rain.

My Father, My Enemy, and My Father

I never could talk to you.
It was like something stuck in my throat:
hysterical bolus.
I, I, I, I

A cold man brave in your smoldering pride,
I used to pray to recover you:
you, you, you, you
who would strangle the mere mention
of your own disappeared father.

Well, you disappeared for me too,
in your sickness, your despair.
You waited too long to try life on your own:
you did not know how old you had grown,
in the thin gut of your self-regard.

And as we walked to the car
I paused a moment to shake your poor hand,
and I said, I guess things will be better
if I see you again
when I meant to say *when*,
or did I?

Something in you shriveled and died
and I did not stop to think
that I might not ever see you again,
nor for years did I believe anything,
except that it was all my fault.

Father, I will have to invent you anew,
in broader, truer strokes,
for your sake,
for mine.

The Legacy
For Judy Lemond

You taught us the fine art
of denial. When your father
abandoned his tribe, you found
your role in life, you became
the one who does not speak of pain.
To us, in our innocence,
this was because you felt
no pain, only emptiness.
Were you ever a child
in his eyes? Was he ever
a god in yours? The day
he disappeared the sky
was torn asunder.
You experienced a loss
that you refused to name,
and so instead of grief
you felt only anger.
Worse still, you hoarded
the anger, you allowed
us none, so we remained
nice boys, nice girls,
cowards all.

It did not take you long
to die, and as usual you had
nothing to tell us. In death
as in life you stayed wrapped
in your cloak of mystery.
In your own way, so sudden
was your departure, you also
abandoned your family,
and you also left behind
a house that was empty,
cold, drab, dreary,
colorless, and full of fears.
Thirty years later we feel
your cold absence, though now
memory serves us better
and much grieving
washes away the sorrow

and the madness.

Sitting Quietly, Doing Nothing

Herring gulls crowd the top of the shed and the wharf
where the fishermen move back and forth
from bucket to black, gut-slimed table.

Behind the house a white cat plays in a field of daisies
and cow vetch, while in the window Mother and I
nurse our coffee and our memories.

The year I was four I ran away with a boy I hardly knew,
across the frozen river to the bright lights on the other
side of town. It was so cold you feared for my life.

The year I was eight a neighbor boy begged me to fight
and I would not, no one knew why. Perhaps, you said,
I was afraid, because of my size, I would hurt him.

The year I was twelve you found me under the bridge,
half asleep, shivering, and still clutching
the weed I'd been smoking.

Sometimes I think you're lucky to be alive, you laugh.
But when I look at what you've made of yourself
I'm sure things have turned out all right.

No, please, Mother, things have not turned out
all right. Can't you see, I've been running,
running, running, all my life.

I love you just as much but I can't
help you anymore. I'm more detached,
now that you've become your own man.

Fine, for once in your life think about yourself,
be a little selfish, take a trip, buy a new hat,
I'm all for that, only remember ...

When I look at you again, your eyes are closed,
your hands are folded, and I know that none
of this is ever again to be broached.

Fed Up
After a poem by Pablo Neruda

Being a mother leaves me cold
that's how it is

I stroll calmly away
drop in at a movie
order cherry cheesecake and coffee
breeze through a shopping mall
buy the most expensive perfume

All I ask is a little vacation from things
from cries and dishes
from gardens and shoelaces
from weekend outings
from report cards
I'd rather not look at them

It so happens I'm fed up
with my feet
and my fingernails
and my face
and my shadow
I don't want to live
like this vacillating
confused chopped up
into bits and pieces
like the news on TV
like the pork loin
in my chili

Yes it would be lovely
to wave a cut lily and panic a cop
or say hell to the crosswalk
and scamper across to yells
and honks it would be nice
just to walk down the street
with a meat cleaver in one hand
raising cane till I die of the shivers

I've had it up to here with catastrophes
I won't go on this way
muddling through
all alone
cold as a corpse
dying of misery
that's why
Monday flees from me
like a cheetah
arching and curling its spine
it's afraid of me

Something shoves me
into damp kitchens
into dark corners
where the workers cower
into shoe stores
where the shoemakers
are drowning in grease
into elevators where everyone
is suddenly tightlipped

I go on crossing offices
fast food chains schoolyards
with the laundry hung out on wires
the shirts and towels and diapers
newly washed slowly dribbling
a slovenly tear

Wings

A loner a drifter you tramp
from place to place seeking
nothing less than the fruit
of the tree of knowledge
under whose limbs you doze
and grow old

Deaf to the cry of the poor
you flee from what might be
and the taste of your own spirit
displeases you

Almost a future
you move towards
blindly
stamping a bit of dirt
still moist from the spade
to dream in a starburst
of vegetables

Its white horses
shimmering
whinnying on high
mounted you soar
above telephone wires
churches shopping malls
beyond the reach
of the dissolute army

To My Brother, On His Serenely Facing Death
For Bill

You let me come along
that day when I was ten
and you were twelve. What choice

did you have? I threatened
to tell Mother and spoil
the joy ride that you'd planned,

with a friend, behind my back,
afraid I'd understand.
Oh but I came walking

up the low hill, barefoot,
with time to kill, stalking
you, brother. In the hot noon-

day sun I could scarcely
be trusted, so sweet the tune,
to hold my tongue. Piss-

ant, you called me, shit-
head, when I insisted
I'd go too, wherever you

were going, or you'd pay.
So we set off, the two
of you hopping mad, tar-

faced me perched, doubled up
with glee, on the handlebars
of your bike, for a ride

into town that took twice
the blood and sweat as otherwise.
Do you remember the name

of the film that was playing?
Something with the word "game."
I remember two things:

the train track we followed
into town, on Sixth, still sings
in my ear; the Sunday

streets, hot, deserted, belonged
to us. And you let me stay
with you in hospital, the time

you were heart-sick. What choice
did you have? The not-so-sublime
truth is that I alone

had neither job nor family
obligations, and partly to atone
for this I agreed to remain.

For that matter, what choice
did I have? To my shame
I had missed Father's

death, and, shit that I was,
Mother's too. If it bothers
you to feel me inside

this room, watching you die,
forgive me, let me ride
with you again, I need

to be present this time:
need to find and read
in the text of your torn

body the hard truth. Why
is there anything born
if, in the end, it comes

to this? In the serene
placement of your arms drums
sound lightly just beyond

these halls, and I have half
my answer. In the fond
familiar tone in which

you ask me, "Who won Reds'
game?" (your drugged voice a bitch
to hear) I have the rest.

To sit with you is no
trouble: some of the best
days of my life I pass

in the dark place between
my breath and yours. The mass-
ive damage to your heart

leaves you with less and less
energy and no more part
to play in the humdrum

lowly world. "It's all right
to let go," I keep hum-
ming in your ear, when I'm

the one, so cold of heart,
unable to find rhyme
or reason to so young

an end. You wait for me,
while every day my tongue
wants a little less of talk,

to find a way to say
good-bye. And when I walk
to the tall trees below

your window, still you wait
for me, and for my soul
to be lifted up. You wait

for me, with labored breath,
when it seems I'll be late
for your death. In the dark

room the red light flashes less
often, my hand, rough as bark,

reaches across to close,

sweet William, one last time,
the vacant eye where glows
no more the light, no more the man.

On the Anniversary of My Mother's Death

I don't miss you as much
as I did then. Twelve years
have gone by, I'm living
alone now, the children
have finished school
and moved away. Sometimes
I want to call you and tell you
what's happening in my life.
I've met a woman, I'm sure
you'd like her. The last time
I saw you I was so unhappy,
so needy I think I frightened
you a little. At the airport
maybe I knew I wouldn't see
you again, I kissed you
and held you until you said
you had to go. I could hear
your flight being called,
and when you disappeared
through the stiff canvas curtains
into security, into the distance
you liked to keep, something
in me did not want to live.

The last time we talked
you were in good spirits,
ready, you said, for whatever
happened. You saw no need
for me to be there, the operation
had a very high chance
of success, something like
ninety percent, your doctor
assured you. Mike
would be there, and Judy,
Bill was going to drive up
from Cincinnati, and anyway
there was nothing I could do
if things didn't work out.
Fool that I was, I listened
to you. Did you think of me,
Mother, in your dying hour?

Did you wish me well?
Did you bless me?

I slept in your bed, the week
of the funeral. I'd wake
before dawn, put on a pot
of coffee, sit at the table
in the kitchen exactly
where you used to sit –
minus the signature cigarette.
To pass the time while the others
slept I read Doris Lessing's
The Golden Notebook –
hardly your cup of tea!
(You preferred solitaire anytime.)
I found the funeral hard to take.
The talk turned too early
and too easily to the notion
that you were safe now,
at peace now, with Dad.
I wanted first to feel
the pain and the loss
and maybe, quite simply,
I needed more time for this
than the others. Back home
I entered a period of silence
and wanting to isolate myself.
A state very close to depression
but definitely not depression, just
a wish to stay away from everyone,
content to sit whole evenings,
not even listening to music,
hardly reading - a psalm
here and there. I became
a passionate swimmer, and found
release in the pool, deep
underwater, in a green
and translucent, womb-like
environment, which took me
back to a time before
the discovery of the world
of pain and sorrow, when
my soul was like a little child,

like a little child *contre sa mère.*

Eve of Destruction

Icy wind
Blowing snow
Grit in my eyes
Betrayed

What She Said

You walk out on me,
You dump everything on me,
The kids, the house, the bills,
Everything, then you expect
Me to have any feeling left,
I'm going crazy but what
Do you care, it's none
Of your concern
From you I get
Nothing, no help,
No understanding,
Nothing.

What makes me
Really angry
Is the way you
Smashed the soapstone
Carving of the medicine
Man with the wings
Of a bird instead of arms
Because it's what I valued
Above everything else
In this sad house.

I've read about men
Like you, with your need
To be always in control.
But that's your problem,
Not mine. I won't play
That game any longer.
I've had enough.
Get out, now.

Coburg and LeMarchant, June 12, 1985

Young woman crossing
In front of me
White summer dress
Red ballet slippers
Her first step hesitant
The right foot
Turned outward
I do not know
Why she started to run
It was not because of me

Sun
For Peter Hutchinson

Ball of fire
sign above
burning the world
into being
and into non-being
in pure interchange
with all things
I bow to you
from mountain tops
from river runs
from forest depths

Blazing ember
beginning and end
of all life
I become for you
a glass
where you shine
through
I am the glass
and I am the one
who polishes the glass
and I am the one
who sees into the glass
with eyes that burn
and itch with the slow
dry desire to see
and seeing to know

Summertime

I love all things cold
again. I love ice
in my wine. I love
stones. Wet, round
stones, from deep
underwater. I love
people with hearts
as cold as arctic
ice. I love them
cold, clean, pure,
isolate in the long,
hot summer's day.

Poetry Slam
For Katie Springer

By the foot of the bed,
from memory, I recite
D'Invilliers' quatrain.
"Then wear the gold hat"
leaves you flat
and you are unmoved.
"If you can bounce high"
brings a smile to your lips
and you are amused.
"Till she cry, Lover"
hits closer to home
and you sigh.

In the window the trees
are yellow and brown.
The harbour is "a blue cove
full of fish processing
and ships that never go
anywhere." With Pound,
the one that begins
"Come, let us pity ..."
all I get is a yawn and
a look of impatience.
"The rich have butlers ..."
sounds so stale, so sixties.
"Dawn enters with little feet ..."
arouses a distant memory
but no feeling and the fine
effect of that final line
with its image of waking
together and sharing
a "clear coolness"
barely registers.

With "Na Audiart" things
begin quickly to come undone.
Image crowds image
with no clear demarcation.
"Thy bodice laces"
rubs against the grain.

"Thy girdle's scope"
weighs heavily in the balance.
Nor do you find aught to praise
in "ivy fingers clutching ..."
The objection you'd raise
is a simple one but fine:
you wish me well not ill
but given one more line
like "being bent and wrinkled"
and you will begin to wonder.

"In an Evil Time" sparks
a real anger, something sharp,
something hitherto unseen.
You can't see how "This is
the night, that was bound to come"
relates to us, to our love.
We are here, we are now,
We have the sun, the sea,
the forest ablaze with colour,
sand dunes where the piping
plover nests in the tall grass,
in the tangles of beach peas.

The bread tastes of thyme
and sage, the cheese
is a Camembert, the wine
a Côte de Rhone,
and I think it's only fair
we have another go at Hesse,
but something light this time,
like "The First Flowers."
Perhaps it's the fragrant wine
Or the fine, moist bread
Or the luscious words
But for some reason you find
"These days so many yellow flowers
have opened their eyes into gold"
not just nice, but right
in tone and thrust.

On the sun-soaked sill
lies the last book

in my bag of surprises,
a beat-up softcover,
Williams's *Immortal Poems*.
"O Mistress mine, where
are you roaming?" I read
at random, and your eyes
sparkle with delight.
"O, stay and hear ..."
breeds more of the same.
But when I come upon
"Your true love's coming ..."
you laugh out loud because,
according to your calculation,
that's a slight exaggeration.
"Once you did and once you
didn't," you're quick to remind me.
But the look in your eyes
tells me that you mean no
harm, and in my heart I rejoice
in that part of you that loves me,
as well as that part that loves
to tease me because they're both
you and you are one and the same.

In the window the trees
are gray and black.
Below the window
the harbour is the back
of a black whale
that connects
this shore
to the far shore.
And when you
draw me down
into a kiss
the words
are mine
and mine alone,
"I live for this
and this alone."

Mary's Point

We happened upon
no sandpiper or plover
at Mary's Point,
but we found
a trembling among
the overarching trees.
We heard
whispering in the trees
instead of birds.
We tasted tears
instead of the lonely
path that all along
we had hungered
never to follow.

The First Seven Days

Thursday we walked on the beach at Cap-Pelé.
After dinner we went upstairs for the first time.
"My bones are like water," you said.

Friday we met in a room behind the bookstore.
We decided not to go to the Aids Benefit Concert.
You left your flannel nightgown in my closet.

Saturday we went to the waterfowl park at dark.
The white, dead trees felt like a Zen rock garden.
I talked of my love for Samuel Beckett.

Sunday you showed me the path to Mary's Point.
When it rained we took shelter under the trees.
We embraced and said we would stay together.

Monday I walked by the chocolate river to your house.
At the bottom of the mud bank stood a great blue heron.
We worked in the garden then celebrated Thanksgiving alone.

Tuesday we watched *Les Enfants du Paradis*.
The way I kissed you brought back a lost memory.
"Many times I have wanted to die," you said.

Wednesday you showed me how to dance the samba.
I read you my poem about Mary's Point.
We made love, slept, made love again.

All evening and night we talked and laughed together.
In the semi-dark your teeth shone like pearls.
"I feel like I'm floating," you said.

In the morning you left early for work.
I could feel you all around me.
My face in the mirror was changed.

C'est ma femme

C'est ma femme,
c'est mon amant
c'est mon amie
c'est mon associé
et c'est une soldate
qui se battait
à mes côtés

The Kiss

She is seen and unseen
jeweled in blue and green
with amethysts and pearls
my lady swirls and swirls

The bed on which she kneels
together with me feels
as when a field in sun
with wildest blooms does run

Her hair is touched with red
her neck with white instead
and all along her spine
there spins a world benign

Where Hall's Creek Flows

Where Hall's Creek flows crosswise
into the wider Petitcodiac
one Sunday morning in mid-October
I saw a great blue heron curled
on one leg, asleep, all alone.
Had I arrived shore-bound
before it woke? Headless,
completely still, it stood
until startled, by a lover
striding grandly, lightly by.
And the flight it then took
in the bright morning sun
was perhaps a "flight from"
but in the lover's eyes
it was seen as a rising,
a soaring, a going home,
a crossing, a return.

All Things Are New: Christmas 1994

The snow is new
The cold wind is new
The ice on the river is new
The lights on Main Street are new
The Baby Jesus in the manger is new
The black trees in the night sky are new
The hoarfrost on the window is new
The fire in the marriage bed is new
The song of the night birds is new
The longing in my heart is new

Starry Night

Behind the house Orion,
diamond-shaped, floats
like a kite, tail down.
Sirius, dog star, shines
brightest, after Venus.
Andromeda lies high
overhead, stretched out.
Flushed from my walk,
I stop a moment behind
the house, enjoying the cold
winter night, while in the warm
window you come and go,
preparing a simple meal,
and singing to yourself.
You make a welcome
for me and still I wait,
remembering other cities,
far-away cities, Lafayette,
Chicago, New York, Halifax,
where I was never at home
the way I am with you.
There is a snow-covered
boot on the back porch,
two candles on the kitchen
table, a pot of soup
on the stove, a bottle
of wine on the counter,
and when I come in
to you, there is a look
in your eyes like distant
stars, and your smile
lights up all my universe.

Three Moons

After a painting by Elaine Amyot

Under a tree, in the light of three moons,
the lovers take shelter. Together they hold
a sort of egg between them that opens
into the one body they share,
the soul-body. In this opening
we see four or five mysterious shapes,
one suggesting a fetus, another a man's
bony fingers, the others too vague
to decipher. In the pond at the foot
of the tree leaves float in water
as white as the moon. The tree
is on a hill that's sacred to lovers
and to the gods of love, to Eros
and to Aphrodite. I know one way
to get there: first blow your horn
as loudly as you know how
and then more loudly still
and when the firebird arrives
don't just stand there, let go,
fly high, forget yourself.

My Hand Upon Your Shoulder
For Rita Auffrey

In the basement of the church after the funeral
of the highly respected executive secretary
of the Maritime Fishermen's Union
and the much loved son brother father
husband and friend to many hundreds
I feel lost in the push and shove of the crowd
until I place my hand upon your shoulder
and feel a sort of grounding work its way
into my arm through my shoulder
into my chest and I'm ready with you to greet
and embrace the widow who only recently
has begun to enter more fully into our lives
because of a mutual interest in poetry
and then to move past her because
so many are behind us in a long line-up
until you and I are next to the table
where many delicious foods are still
untouched and many new thoughts
remain unsaid without needing to be said
and with my hand again upon your shoulder
I am strangely happy to be here and happy
to be among this throng of people this company
keeping watch with the widow and the mother
and the son and the brothers and the lost man's
many friends who once walked upon the same water.

Halfway to the Millennium

I see a blue heron rising –
the S of its neck straightening –
and over the river, darkness.

I see a red woman standing –
in a field of tulips and daisies –
and behind, a coiled snake.

I see a crow tottering –
the limbs of the tree quaking –
and below, the beloved.

I see a black man walking –
skirting the edge of the cliff –
and beyond, the abyss.

Changing of the Guard

The first time we made love
we were delicate
as snails
shy
as moose
quiet
as fish
crafty
as foxes
glad
as geese

Now when we make love
we are rough
as swans
proud
as horses
loud
as crows
careless
as raccoons
happy
as harp seals

If You Are Waiting For Anything
After a construction by Elaine Amyot

This piece of old bark
is the torso of a woman
big-bellied woman
with black dots
the size of pinholes
scattered all around,
bulges that could be
scallop shells,
and other pieces
tiny as thumbnails
white as moonbeam
attached to the main body
like fragments of a dream,
layered, ancient, and rough.
Above the bark
is a paper-thin remnant
or segment of a wasp's nest,
cone shaped, gray,
with a fluted hole at the top.
This is the head of the woman.
It's tilted to the right,
and so thin, so delicate
that if I touch it it breaks
and crumples. Already
in places it's broken.
The figure stands to one side,
with a query no one
can remember anymore.
Or maybe it's not
a woman's torso
but a breastplate,
and the scallop shells
are where the breasts
would be fitted.

Big-bellied woman,
wife, lover, wasp-mother,
you have been here in your box
for such a very long time,
just yourself,

making no demands,
quiet, self-reliant,
there was something
almost pitiful in that
which I did not want
to acknowledge.
Only lately have I begun
to hear a buzzing
around my head,
and only lately
has it dawned on me
that you've been busy
with your own dreams,
your own stories,
your own pain,
and that if you are waiting
for anything from me,
it is for me to be born.

Yesterday I Thought Winter

Yesterday I thought winter
was here to stay, and I went about
making ready, shaking out
the down-filled jacket, rubbing oil
into the black leather boots, digging deep
into the drawer for the sheepskin
hat that lets me walk anywhere –
onto the marsh or into town –
without dread of the icy wind.
It was already dark when
I got home, and you were late,
having stopped to see a friend
after school. We ate leftover
lentil soup, Nick the Dutch Baker's
Russian rye bread, and we drank
a toast to winter, we said
there's no season we love better –
or worse for that matter –
but winter means we gather
supplies like squirrels,
we prepare a shelter,
we light candles,
we build a fire,
we remember
long neglected friends,
children who've grown
apart, parents all sadly
dead. It means that we
rejoice all the more
in our being together,
and we remember times
when we were not,
when we were alone,
and we try not to forget
the many who still are.
We agree with the Greeks
that it's wise not to count
any man or woman
happy till (s)he is dead.

Yesterday I thought winter

was here to stay, and I went
outside into the snow, fat, wet
flakes on my face, and I saw
a white mist over the marsh
and a white gull gliding low
over the water, and I wept
to see the briny water flow.

From the Bridge at Hall's Creek

Dizzy from my walk
not what I once was
whale of a man
I wait on the bridge
above muddy water
come springtime
and the banks begin
to thaw and loosen
the river empties
and deepens
but still the salmon
come our way
no longer

Across the marsh
at Dover Settlement
in a flutter of eyelids
the hills glow
and the river glows
like silver
and blood flows
to the brain
liltingly
the eyes water
the subject dissolves
into the object
like afternoon clouds
dissolve in sunshine

At Shepody Mills
the water rises
and falls rises
and falls
the waves
tell a tale
of longing

Return to Grand Manan

The island hides itself
from prying eyes. The fog
is sometimes so massive
that nothing can be seen,
not even a gull. On the deck
behind the Inn we can hear
water lapping the stone-infested
beach. Bell buoys clang
and clang again. Across the bay
children play by the hotel
swimming pool, their voices
raised to a steady high pitch,
interrupted every now and then
by a squeal like some animal
caught under a car's wheel.

Below the deck the lawn
is a riot of wildflowers –
hawkweed, purple clover,
blue flag, daisies, and wild lupine.
Farther down, near the cliff,
there's a tent with tables inside,
where you can sit, drink a beer,
and watch the boats as they move
into the shelter of the wharf.
Passengers in life jackets line
the decks, and as we walk
to the edge of the cliff,
they wave to us like old friends.

Beyond the beach a boardwalk
crosses the bog to where the more
exotic flora are to be found –
the pitcher plant and the carnivorous
sundew. Halfway across, the sky
opens and the rain comes pouring
and pelting down. Always before
after making love we've said
all's right with the universe,
but now, the way the bad news
seems to follow us everywhere,

even here to the island, we're
not so sure, the world's mad,
and our words, no matter how close
we guard them, ring hollow.

Aboard the boat, just offshore,
the island is even more impressive,
with its lonely beaches, its high bluffs,
its ancient rock. And as we move out
into the bay the fog becomes thinner,
and the light has a golden white quality
that's as delicate as a Turner.
Another ship drifts nearby,
appearing and disappearing
in the fog, then appearing
a second time, with its sails down,
like a ghost ship from long ago.
The sea is calm, the air warm,
and harbor porpoises swim
close by as we tack into water
that's as smooth as silk,
brought around again, the way
the wind will bring a ship around,
to the feeling that everything,
if just for this one moment,
is happening as it should.

Low Water

Farther down
the dark
slippery stones
and the tidal
pools
harboring
life in miniature
and still farther
down
and there
under
the sculpted rock
a man
lights a cigarette
and he does not
care
if the tide
covers him
now
or later

At Parrsboro
we walked
as far out
as we could
below
the lighthouse
and I listened
to the water
rushing out
and I saw
a boy
and a girl
run barefoot
in the mud
and I was
alone

Sometimes
where I live
the mud banks

are blue
sometimes
bright as silver
when you
are gone
I sit
and stare
at the clay
jug
on the table
and it's not
your face
I see
but mountain
tops
pine trees
and below
all seven
oceans
and the maker
of the oceans
and mountains
while I wait
for you
like a fisherman's
wife
waits for the tide
to come in
waits for it
to wash over me
making me
smooth
and clean
again
like stones
on a beach
see how
they weep.

Waiting To Be Born

In the morning when I'm high
and the sky's the limit
and I'm giving birth
to poems and plays
I've put off for days
and weeks
it's then that I hatch
wild schemes to win
your wayward heart

At noon in the room below
I hear you singing
softly to yourself
and the music
and the words
renew
my appetite
for life

In the afternoon flat
on my back in bed
I'm waiting to be born
inside a hollow time
where no one is going
anywhere and nothing
remains but a pounding
and a whirling
from which there is
no escaping

At close of day when I'm low
and time grows so heavy
I don't want go on living
then the thought of you
washes over me
like the ocean
washes over stones
on a beach cleansing
and polishing
ancient debris

I Sometimes Forget

I sometimes forget, after ten years of marriage,
how much I love you. Forgetting is a fruit
I crave, an emptiness. In the fall we gather
the dry, yellow leaves.

I can go for weeks standing just outside
your door, listening to you. The notes you sing
are soft, white worry beads. On the shore
above the river we build a fire.

How many times have I seen you hiding
your breasts, your sex. The curve of your flank
is the shape of my desire. We sleep and wake
to voices in the next room.

Lifted out of time we stride the earth
Like giants. Loving you is the brush stroke
that quickens the floating world. In winter
we rise with the first light.

On Becoming Canadian

The program says there are forty-three
new citizens from twenty-three countries
but not a single one has thus far come forward
to join me in the front row. It's feeling
pretty cold and lonely here. I have the words
to "Oh Canada" in both official languages,
a veterans of foreign wars handout,
an information package from the Multicultural
Association of the Greater Moncton Area,
and a greeting card from The Catholic
Women's League, and that's not all.
I read everything once, then again,
I get up and greet all my friends,
I take my turn at the back of the room
to sign the oath of allegiance
but even after all that is done
I find I'm still sitting alone
in the front row, sticking out
like a sore thumb, and feeling
that I've been too clever by half,
coming early to grab the best seat.

From the back of the room a mounted
policeman steps forward, in full regalia,
followed by the judge, a small, tough-as-nails
Acadian woman, our local member of parliament,
also Acadian, but larger, famous for her bear hugs
and her work for the poor, and the district supervisor
for Citizenship Canada, as well as several town officials.
The ceremony is set to begin and suddenly
it's clear to me that I cannot sit here
alone, ill-at-ease, unable to enjoy
this pomp and this circumstance.
And so I'm on my feet, bent over,
doubling back, ducking down
into the empty seat in row three,
next to a man I hardly know,
who's also an American,
though a much more recent arrival.
Good luck, we say to each other
and all at once there's a gravity

to the proceedings I hadn't expected,
as one by one, beginning with the letter
"A", our names are called and we rise
and go to the front of the room,
exchange a few words with the judge,
shake hands with Claudette,
receive a miniature flag
and continue on down the line.
It's this movement forward,
people from twenty-three countries,
every race, every culture,
moving forward, and the sense
that Canada is a country that chooses,
every day, against the odds,
to move forward, not backward,
to be as inclusive as it can be,
not closing the door to so many,
as it seems my native land
is hell-bent on doing.

I'm not nervous when my turn
approaches, because I know
I'm doing the right thing
at the right time, and because
there are so many friends here
who are glad for me,
and because my wife
is signaling to me,
index finger touching her lips,
that she has a kiss for me
on my way back to my seat.
And I'm not cutting all ties,
it's more like I'm entering
into something, rather than
leaving something behind.
I am a citizen now
in this new country,
Canada, my voice
matters.

Dog On Retreat

At night while we sleep a dog
roams the monastery grounds
like a phantom. In the morning
I listen for his name to be called
but for now Boy will suffice,
or Hey Now. Full of youthful
energy, he wants to keep moving,
always moving, and if I go with
him where he wants me to go,
I have neither time nor desire
to stop and meditate, to sit
and do nothing. He is here now,
Boy, Hey Now, apparently,
to work against such desire.

The surface of the lake is smooth
and still where it spills over the dam
and down a wide, flat concrete surface,
running fast and clear to the edge,
the lip a brown, dirty jet of water,
a trickle or a torrent depending
on the rains. Boy, Hey Now,
crosses the footbridge over the dam
then comes back when he sees
I am not following. The water
below the dam swirls and foams
before forming a brook that flows
into the woods, toward the road
that borders the monastery grounds.
A path through the woods ends
in a tangle of moss-covered stones
near where the water, black now,
ripples under the road, through
a ten-foot-high metal conduit.
The earth rises to form a cliff face,
some fifty feet high, the rocks
long and flat, layered, as if stacked
carefully by hand. All up and down
the rock face leaves have fallen
and clung, autumn leaves, wet
and glistening, from the birch trees

perched precariously above, their limbs
hiding and revealing the sky.

Boy, Hey Now, slips down
into the water, curious to know
more about this new gurgling thing,
and for a moment he's swept along.
A rock breaks free from the cliff
and falls into the water, the bells
from the monastery ring out,
the silence is broken, and Boy,
Hey Now, scrambles back,
and runs ahead, along the rushing
brook, while I linger, glad
to be alone, until I'm sure
everyone is inside, at chapel.
But when I come up the hill
I am surprised to see Boy,
Hey Now, galloping toward
the door where the monk
is waiting, calling his name
and scattering scraps of food
on the pavement with a simple
motion of the arm, embracing
the dog's wild exuberance.

Barrington Street, Halifax
For Irmi Lenzer

North on Barrington the sidewalks
are nearly empty and when I see you
in the window of the used book store
I can hardly believe it's you.
The last time I wrote
I said something in anger
and you did not respond.
You've retired in the meantime
and moved to an undisclosed location
and even the children
no longer write. Did you
poison them against me?
But there I go again.
I said I would write
out of love because ultimately,
every poem is a love poem.
It can be about sorrow
or anger or hate,
but if it is not written out of love
it will fail as a poem.

A book in the window
has caught your attention,
and you are lost in thought.
You raise your left hand
as I approach until it almost
covers your face. With your fingers
you seem to be rubbing something
into being or into non-being.
Absent the familiar profile
I cannot be sure it is you
until I'm at your side,
and the startled look you give me
is the same look you gave me
the very first time I ever saw you,
at university, in a laboratory, punching
the ears of rats. In answer to my question
you point to the book that has interrupted
your journey through Halifax streets –
Rilke's *Book of Hours*.

On the cover there's a photograph
showing intense rays of light
shining through tall trees.
The first book we ever read together
was Rilke's *Sonnets to Orpheus*.
I'd like to tell you about the book
I'm reading now, but before I can begin
you are walking away, and I find myself
running to catch up with you.

I wanted to write a poem
about love, a love large enough
to include sorrow, anger, even hate.
But I think it is already too late,
and you have no desire
to listen to me any longer.
At the light you stop
and look at me – your eyes
were always your most
remarkable feature –
and I want you to know
that I've never stopped
loving you. All you can do
is shake your head, and your words,
when you do speak, are softer
than I can ever remember,
soft as the pine needles
on the floor of the forest
the day Rilke went walking
and the light came streaming
down. Because you think
the only person I've ever loved
is myself, and with these words,
for which I have no answer,
you are gone and I'm standing
alone at the corner of Barrington
and Sackville
and I'm wondering why
deep inside me
and all around me
all I feel
is this intense
glow.

Love Poem to My Brother on His Failing to Remember My Name
For Bob

What I always loved about you is that you were not shy about being
emotional. You said what you felt and I could believe you.
You would take the initiative in making contact.
And you didn't take yourself too seriously, you could laugh
at yourself. So when you began to forget words and I could feel
your desperation in searching for the word you could still laugh
at yourself, and at your quandary. Fatigue and stress
have taken their toll, they plague you like
horseflies plague a wounded animal, plunging
in and out of woods, falling into bogs, finally unable
to move. When I'm talking with you on the phone there comes
a moment of silence and I hear you turning to your wife
and she has to tell you the word and I suppose it's almost as bad
as times when a wife has to change a husband's diapers.
Fatigue and stress are the twin causes everyone tells you and you can go along
with this diagnosis, though it doesn't go very deep. But the other day
when you were trying to talk about this you could not remember
the word 'stress' and I could hear the anguish in your voice
as you dug for what was no longer there. I tried to help
but you said it's all right and you wanted to say my name
but you could not remember it and I had to tell you. What I always loved
about you is that you did not hide your emotions and so I try to be
a little bit like you, and I struggle to find the words to tell you I love you.

Something Happened
For Anna

You wanted to be where it was happening, where
great events would change the course of history and
nothing would ever be the same. You were in
Montreal, for instance, when it looked like the
country was about to tear itself apart – you
wanted to see what that would be like. Later, when
you were living in Vancouver, you crossed the border in
buses to see just how ugly Seattle could get, with
props in place, cameras rolling, and the
whole world watching. When I was your age and I
wanted everything turned upside down, I'd
go away for a while, or I'd change careers, or I'd meet some
one new, or somebody would die ... it was all so much easier.

We get thrown into the world, say the philosophers, and
if this is true, you made the best of a bad situation, by
throwing yourself at events – as observer, participant, and
(later) reporter. Even before you knew you wanted to be a
journalist, you had the instincts of a journalist, the
same way that a future film-maker might walk a
way from her friends, toward the end of the beach, rather than
stay and listen to some boy telling dirty jokes around the fire.

It seemed only natural, in the spring of 2001, just after
university, that you would choose New York City, be
cause New York City was where the next big thing was most like
ly to happen. What you hadn't counted on was being so close by when
it did happen, and you had not imagined that it would take the
form that it did. Exiting your office at the Village Voice, and
turning north to escape the smoke and the flames, you
felt rather than saw the first building fall, and if
I can quote you here, from something that
you wrote a few days later, incomprehensible
thunder cracked inside you and shook the
screams of thousands now clogging the streets.

Something happened that I don't yet
understand. Even several years after the event you
don't want to see me, or talk to me. It's as if when those
workers trapped on the upper floors threw themselves from the

windows, you threw yourself into a new way of looking at things and you subsequently found it impossible or unseemly to share this with me. Walking away from the stricken towers, you were also walking away from me.

According to Plan

Black smoke – In the distance –
The doomed city – Burns –
At the checkpoint – A mix-up –
A failure to communicate –
Soldiers panic – Ten dead –
Seven children –
According to plan.

Winter storm – With no let up –
The driving snow – Turns –
To freezing rain – Limbs –
Of trees – Bend –
To the ground – The mail –
Cannot get through –
According to plan.

Civilian deaths – As routine –
As breakfast – Flitter –
Across the screen –
A health scare – Steals –
The headlines – Tired –
We turn away –
According to plan.

Afternoon sun – As warm –
As spring – Daggers glitter –
In every tree – Every bush –
Where water drips down –
Beauty – All around –
And danger –
According to plan.

Before the Fire

Before the fire the tower
was Romanesque, ten
stories of pink granite,
the roof slanted
more steeply than perfidy.

The moment the sun
struck the face of the clock,
something happened, a death,
many deaths, and I could hear
voices whispering in my ear.

The sky darkened,
and the rain began to fall,
on the pavement and on me,
as I walked, head down,
towards the graveyard.

My Home Town

There are no skyscrapers
in my home town,
and everywhere I go
I can see the blue hills.
When the sun shines
the downtown comes alive
with bars and cafés
filled to overflowing.
Our tidal river,
like our troubled past,
seldom rises now
to flood our minds.
People in my home town
are interested in music,
theatre, literature and dance.
The powers that be
are friendlier here
and I am less
an outsider.
On a hillside
at the edge of town
an ecological park hides
more treasures
than it reveals.
I have no desire
to go south
for the winter.

My Wife

There is nothing like
your body,
it has a fullness
that is revealed only
to me.
On the darkest day
your laughter
is like a flame
that flickers
but will not die.
When you go through the streets
no one recognizes you,
no one but me.
In your winter coat and hat
arm in arm with a friend
you are marching through the snow
for global warming.
In your studio
beside an unfinished
canvas
you are fielding questions
from a journalist.
In the backyard
with the pond as backdrop
you are surrounded
by your children
and grandchildren.
I am less alone now
than I was
before I met you.
I will give you
no reason
to be angry with me
ever again.
I do not see
an end
to our life together.

Old Age

People know me,
what I've done,
who I am.
I'm free
to give things away
with no regrets,
no second thoughts.
I'm glad to have
some money
in my pocket.
In folding chairs
at the end of the dock
I keep my granddaughter
company,
and though we barely know each other
we are happy.
On my morning walk
by the river
I kneel
to embrace a dog
who's just as much a stranger
to me
as I am to him.
At the bottom of the street
my wife and I stop
to admire
the ice sculpture
that appeared,
miraculously,
overnight.
I do not believe
that my children
think so little of me.
I do not want
recognition
for the work I've done.
I do not want
to have sex
with younger women.

Man Waving His Arms in a Field

Just beyond the clump of apple trees,
where the ground dips and rises again,
you hold forth every day, delivering
a solitary rant. From the house
we can see you waving your arms,
and we can hear you too,
when you turn toward us
and raise your voice.
We'd like you to let it be,
get on with your life – as if you had a life.

Farther back in the woods,
in another, long-neglected field,
lies the ancestral burial ground,
and it's decided at a family meeting
to re-bury Father, without
all the fuss and ceremony.
You are against it in the beginning.
You like Father where he is.
You are not done with your list of grievances.
There is still much that he has to answer for.
But your brothers and their wives,
their children too – those old enough to care –
have had enough. The second field
will be different, we tell you,
because it is far from the house,
and the memories will be more distant.

It's not easy getting Father
out of the ground and onto the rickety wagon.
The trail through the woods, linking the first
and the second fields, needs clearing,
and branches keep snapping back,
scratching our faces. We frighten
a few animals along the way – blue jays,
partridges, crows, a nest of squirrels.
The noise of the tractor, the cracking of limbs
under the wheels, is like music to your ears,
drowning out your dark mutterings.

You do not visit Father as often as before,

and when you do, you bring something,
an offering, perhaps the branch of a tree
that you stumbled across on the way,
or wildflowers that you gathered in the first field.
You speak to him, but softer now,
and after you've spoken you stay awhile,
listening to the crows calling
back and forth, the cars
on the road that winds
invisibly through the hills,
the wind in the trees that rattles
the leaves of the birch trees
but does not disturb the spruce,
the fir, or the apple trees.
You remain silent until a deer
steps out of the woods,
or a hummingbird flutters
near your shoulder,
or a memory floods
your mind, of the way
Father held his hands,
fingers together, thumbs splayed,
when he lifted you up to the first limb
of the first tree you ever climbed.

Frogman at Break of Day

Green knitted house slippers
on the steps. Count to ten.
Hold on to the window sill.
It's still dark. Dream images
flicker and fade. Keep going.
Turn up the heat. Let the cat
out. Start the coffee.
Birdsong in the window.
Listen to the crows
in the trees. Swallow
last night's bitter
after-taste. Breathe
in and out. Sip
coffee. Get comfortable.
Notice the light falling
across the back of the chair
and the way the rungs
glow. Embrace the
solitude, and the promise
of the end of solitude.
Let go of all thoughts
that otherwise would float
dimly in the shadow
of their own insignificance.
Wait for the sound
of your feet on the steps,
the sensation of your lips
on my lips.

We Have a Past

The building looks run-down,
in need of painting.
Let's don't go in.
Let's find another place to lunch.
We stopped here once,
a year into our marriage,
and it was sweet then.
The dining room in the basement
was labyrinthine, the service
and the menu both outstanding.
On the way to our room
we admired, on a landing
by the stairs, the owner's
collection of cameras.
But that was then.
Let's find another place to lunch.

The crowd for the concert
is smaller than expected.
The floors have been sanded,
polished and stained
since the last time we were here.
The pews are cushioned.
After the concert we stroll
across the hillside,
looking down upon the wide,
deceptively calm tidal river.
The mud banks reflect
the purple of the evening sky.
We picnicked here,
many years ago,
in the grass above the river,
at the edge of the dirt road.
It was a weekday,
and we were alone
except for the ghosts
that haunted the graveyard
above the church.

The house where we live
is the same house

where we've always lived,
and yet it's not the same.
We've dug a pond.
We've built a deck.
We've planted a garden.
We've painted and repainted.
The roof is new.
The basement no longer leaks.
The cats we love
are not the same cats we loved
ten years ago.
The friends we see
are not the same friends we saw
when we were married.
The sounds we make
are not the same sounds we made
when we first made love.
The past slips away
into forgetfulness,
and it thickens there,
like the bird droppings
on some south sea island,
buried so deep
we cannot remember.
But sometimes,
when we least expect it,
a fragment of that past
will come flying at us
and force us to stand
and fight for our lives.

The Universe We Inhabit

Every time we make love
it's like the first time.

"My bones are like water,"
echoes over the years.

The universe we inhabit
is a floating universe.

What is above and what is below
are in balance.

They mirror each other,
and we are reflected back.

When it rains we take shelter
under the trees.

Overheard

You have been so patient all these years
while we pretended you were not there.
At Thanksgiving, at Christmas, at weddings,
funerals, graduations, every August
when we rented a cottage by the sea,
we carried on as if you did not exist.
And you seemed content, until recently,
to play along with this fiction.

If you had come knocking at the door
or if you had called us and told us
that you had no place to go
of course we'd have welcomed you.
But perhaps you were too shy,
perhaps you felt you did not know us well enough.
Truth be told, we knew that you were listening;
that's what gave our conversation
whatever spice and energy it had:
we were not just talking to ourselves
but, through you, to the larger world.

In the old photographs there is always someone
there in the background, unknown to us,
who never minded being ignored.
You were happy to listen,
to observe, to bide your time.
At least such is the message
we all believed
you wanted us to hear.

Portrait of a Woman on a Train

In the space between the seats the woman
seems young, not twenty. Her face
is painted to make her look older,
and she's wearing a hat that fits
tightly over her forehead and ears.
They are running away together,
to Arizona, California, Mexico.
She has had to leave everything,
friends, parents, belongings, and
she's worried, she's scared, but
it's too late. In the beginning,
when the man confided in her,
it was all so exciting. But now,
with him calling the shots,
in his striped suit and bow tie,
his pipe and his devil-may-care
attitude, she's not so sure. And
what about the wife he's leaving
behind? What about the children?
Along the curve of her neck
there's a brown fuzz so fine
it turns the skin to gold. I could love
this girl, given half a chance,
I could run away with her, no
problem. But where would I go
if I left home? Would I even care?
I'd say, the devil made me do it,
I'd say, the devil's real too,
try him if you dare.

Portrait of My Grandfather as a Boy and as a Grown Man

His two older siblings look sure of themselves,
steely-eyed, hard-nosed. But he, Edward Aden,
dressed up like a little monkey, squeezed
into clothes that are too small, has a lost, scared,
defiant look. If he is entertaining dark thoughts,
which he almost certainly is, he is keeping them
to himself. Later, when he is Fred Clancy's age,
or Minnie Mae's, he'll find a mask that fits.
In the one picture I have of him as a grown man
he is outdoors, cleaving to his wife and five
children in a clearing in the woods,
the ground soft with a scattering of autumn leaves.
He is a short, plump, pleasant-looking man,
dressed in black trousers and a white shirt,
with the sleeves rolled up, his gaze
directed not at the camera or his wife,
or any of his five children, but at something
behind the camera, which he alone can see.

Portrait of My Grandmother

She is not tall but she is big –
big arms, big bosoms, big hips.
She is turned with her back to me,
her left arm out, the elbow tucked
neatly into my midsection. Though
I'm only fifteen I tower over her,
in my jeans, my white T-shirt, and
my black and white shoes. Her forearm
and hand are as big and as strong
as a man's, bigger than my brother's,
who is standing to her right,
his arm laid nicely against her shoulder
and breast. Behind us, framing us,
is a corner of the house and one post,
in sunlight, of the veranda. She's wearing
a long summer dress with some sort of belt
at the waist. Black leather boots or shoes
in shadow. I see Father's eyes in her eyes,
and his nose – a large, fleshy nose.
She has the straight-ahead, frank look
of a woman used to being obeyed.
When she says something, people listen
or get out of the way. No wonder
Her husband, my grandfather, thought
he would die, if he stayed longer under
the same roof. She kept getting bigger, year
after year, while he, the man of the house,
kept getting smaller. Already he was
smaller than his oldest son. A small, plump
man who made no impact, he'd walk
into his own house, and look around,
and it was as if he were not there.
The woman's voice was heard,
his ignored. To disappear, to run,
seemed like the easiest thing to do.

Portrait of My Father as Den Father

A field with ruts and bare spots.
Woods in the back. Fred and I
are the only ones not in uniform.
Father, in a bulky sweater and
a shirt with a white collar,
looks straight at the camera.
A strong wind musses his hair.
He stands firm and solid,
a father among fathers, his two boys
the tallest of those gathered in the half circle.
Why did he not continue in the role
of den father beyond the one year
I can remember, when I must have been
nine or ten? Was he too busy with work?
Did he dislike the outdoors?
Or was it something else? Was it
that he did not like the loud ways
of young boys? Whatever happened
to that look of joy? Did fatherhood
become so much a burden to him
that he stopped feeling anything
other than the worry and the anger?
Or did he simply stop letting me
be part of it? Did he forget me?
If you can hear me now, Father,
Listen to me, Hold your child
and be glad. It is not your job
to carry the weight of the world
on your shoulders, just carry
your child, lift him high.

Portrait of a Man Reading

At the table under a bare lightbulb
he sits alone, his eyes downcast,
waiting. A pocket book lies on the table
in front of him, unopened. The illustration,
in color, shows a prospector, rifle in hand,
leading a pack mule through scrub hills.
The title has the word "Tappan" in it.
Read a page out loud, I urge him,
and to my surprise he obliges.
His voice is a whisper, not the deep,
rough voice I had expected,
and the words he speaks are barely
decipherable. As he sets the book down
silence again envelops the room, like
autumn ice across a New England pond.
At the sink he fills a glass with cold tap
water, shuffles past me into the hallway,
and down the hallway into the living
room, where he sits in a rocking chair
before the flickering screen,
with no one to keep him company,
too tired to read, too restless to sleep.
He raises and lowers his hands, slowly,
methodically beating the backs of the hands
against his thighs. Nothing but this
rocking back and forth, this steady
rhythm, can comfort him now.
He sits alone in the dark room,
and I can feel his power
steadily ebbing.

Portrait of a Family Manqué

On the running board of a car we sit,
side by side, Fred, myself, and Charlie.
Our sister, Ellen, stands nearby,
against the high, rounded front fender.
Some distance off, near a second car,
stands Father, with a hose in his hand.
We seem to be looking uphill toward
Father, though this is likely an illusion.
Charlie, with his pudgy hands around
his knee, and his head is turned
toward the camera, is the only one
not looking toward Father. Fred,
sitting between Ellen and me,
has his hand placed gently
on Ellen's shoulder. She seems
to be moving off toward Father,
and Fred is holding her back,
or telling her, Steady as she goes.
The way we sit on the running board,
and the angle of the photo, taken
from below, close to ground level,
means we do not even come up
to the door handle, while Father,
not far off, is huge, his head
jutting over the church a block away.
The sun is in Charlie's eyes,
and the way he's set his jaw,
forward, gives him a hard look,
unsuited for one so young.

Portrait of My Sister Ellen

A veranda, low to the ground,
with white columns across the front,
each column a slender cone set high
on cement blocks. In front of the veranda,
in the grass, my sister poses for a photograph
with Mother, both of them dressed for church,
in their best clothes, including light-colored
coats and hats. A shrub bush, the same height
as Mother, fills the space just behind where
they stand. Mother has her left hand placed
gently on Ellen's shoulder, and she's leaning
forward, as if she's not quite sure if she's
going toward or away from her daughter.
Both have the same happy, quiet smile.
From the evidence of the picture Ellen
likes the Mother she has, though now
she'd have believe that this, like so much else,
was never really the case. Is it that the picture
gives us a false impression? Search as I may,
I can find nothing false in it. Ellen, I see,
is holding something in her hand. A figure
hangs on a string that is wound about her thumb.
It looks like a finger puppet – a gingerbread man.
In any case, a figure of some kind. She stands
so straight and tall, and seems so happy.
Is it Mother who makes her happy?
Or is it the little friend she holds,
tenderly, self-consciously, on a string?

Portrait of a Girl with Backpack

A girl is coming up the road,
a nylon backpack on her back,
the straps tight around her broad,
strong shoulders. She gets taller
and taller as she approaches, until
she's within an inch of my own height.
A few feet away she stops and waits,
and I am not sure if she is waiting
for a friend to catch up with her,
or for me to explain myself. But
I have no words of explanation,
which brings a smile to her face.
She's dyed her hair red, her lips
are black, her eyes are so clear
and penetrating I look away,
intimidated. The house I want
is on Henry Street, she says,
in answer to a question I've yet
to compose. It's a blue house
with a lilac bush in front. A man
lives there with his son, who's
shall we say a little odd. Arms
out, like wings, skipping,
dancing in circles, the girl
moves up the hill, while I,
transfixed, remain behind.

Portrait of the Artist in Her Studio
For Nancy King Schofield

The studio is in an old barn,
on the floor above where the animals,
the farm equipment, and the hay
are kept. She has everything
she needs – a bed to sleep in,
electricity to run her power tools
as well as boil water, a miniature
fridge to keep things cold, table
and chairs in case company comes,
a chemical toilet so she does not
have to run to the main building
every time, a hoist attached
to the side of the building, to lift
heavy tools and pieces of stone,
and a talkative horse in the room
below to keep her from feeling lonely.
At the top of the stairs as we enter
the studio, the artist has hung a piece
of plywood, ten feet by twelve,
which she has painted, gouged,
painted some more, and festooned
with cast-off bolts, nuts, and sections
of an old band-saw to demonstrate
that nothing is ever completely lost
or abandoned. The paint is the same
dark rust-brown as the cast-off metal,
with a hint of red, and what she says
is indubitably true, it *is* dismal.
But then she always says the same thing
about her works on plywood, and she
keeps coming back to them, like a bee
to sweet marjorem. At the other end
of the room there'd a huge piece of limestone,
seven or eight feet tall, cylindrical,
with the faint suggestion of arms pressed
close to the sides, but nothing else as yet.
The stone, though un-worked, has a beautiful
coloring, a light yellow, as if it were coming
from within. On the floor are two rusted
metal rings that one day, presumably,

will encircle the stone, like belts.
And when, at last, we sit at the table
for a cup of tea, we can hear the horse
on the floor below, moving about,
clomp, clomp, clomp, bumping
into things, kicking and snorting.

Portrait of a Museum Goer
On viewing Seurat's 'Sunday Afternoon on the Island of La Grande Jatte'

It's a large canvas, over ten feet across,
and this in itself is a jolt. To get close
is to go into this altogether too balanced,
too calm, too harmonious scene. It makes
the viewer dizzy, the way everyone is lost
in his or her own world, inwardly sealed off.
There's one couple near the center, the woman
with her arms up, around the man's neck,
and that's nice. Is he looking at her? His head
is bent, turned to one side. No, he is looking
at me, the viewer who happened by.
All the energy in the picture is sucked
right out of it, where his eyes betray
his apathy. There's nothing alive
in this painting, except the seven trees
in the upper right-hand corner that burn
with a fire that captures the imagination.
Is this an accident of coloration?
It helps, I think, that we get away
from the human element and move
into something dark and unformed.
In the dark a light glows and this,
for now, is enough.

Portrait of the Night Clerk

In a long, flowery, loose-fitting dress
with no shoulders, she is better attired
for a dinner out than for a job as clerk
at a motel. Getting up from her chair
behind the desk she winces, and something
between a sigh and a moan escapes her lips.
She lifts one shoulder then the other while
looking at me, her tardy, late-night guest.
She seems glad to have a chance to get up
and move about. She's been sitting too long,
reading her book. She glances at my name
on the registration form, and pronounces
it incorrectly. Nonplussed, I ask hers.
"Sandy," she says. "Nice name for a night
clerk at a motel, eh?" I have to laugh,
"Don't need no sand in these eyes tonight,
thank you very much." The door opens
and in flies Sandy's boyfriend, all pumped,
in a green crew-neck undershirt that has
Blast Off written across the front in white.
He greets me as if he's known me all
his life. "I'll get *monsieur* here his keys
and then I'll be ready," the words flow
from your lips. Ready for what, I'd
like to ask, as I go in search of my
room, which lies at the end
of the building, where I have
a view of the city in the distance.
I park my car, a Saturn, ass backwards
up against the door, though for the love
of God I don't know for what reason,
for I have nothing to unpack except
my loneliness and my lust.

Birthday in October
Poem for Kimberly Gautreau

October
when nature
shuts down
and snow
and ice
foreshadow
earth's mysterious
turning-within
when fall's
colors fade
and we frail
human beings
amounting to little
in the scheme of things
embrace
what light remains
and kindle
a thousand flames

Because You Were Not Beautiful

Because you were not beautiful
your parents did not make a fuss
over you at Christmas and on birthdays
the way they did with your sister
and your brother believing you
were not worth the extra effort

Because you were fat
you were the last girl
to get invited to the dance
and it turned out that the boy
didn't really like you very much
though you liked him well enough
because he was the only one

Because you were gruff
and cut your hair short
your husband said he couldn't
live with you any longer
even though you had two children
who cried for him constantly

Because you couldn't stand
the singles scene
and because you didn't have a picture
that you dared post on the net
on one of those dating sites
because you were not beautiful
you were home the night
your best friend called you
from her cell phone sobbing
because her husband had hit her
and she had nowhere to go
and you were able to take her in
and give her a place to sleep
and a shoulder to cry on
and she said you were the most
beautiful person she'd ever known

Homage to One Who Lived His Life
After a poem by John Meagher

You never wrote a poem or painted a picture
but your life was a work of art.
I can easily see you
at your desk, firing off e-mails
in the name of your beloved fisherman's union
whenever you felt an injustice needed addressing.
Whenever you got really excited
you'd wave your arms in the air
like an orchestra conductor,
and oh, how I admired you then!
But though you were a fierce advocate
you were also a peacemaker,
the one who was called upon
whenever things got ugly,
as they did for example a few years ago
when the native and the non-native
fishermen near Burnt Church
just couldn't find a way to live together.
What kept you grounded was your love
of animals. You loved all animals
but especially dogs. Not just your own
dog but all dogs, even wild dogs.
The first time I ever saw you
was at the scene of an accident,
where a car had run over a dog
and the dog lay mortally injured.
I saw you bend over the dog,
place your hand on her shoulder,
and whisper something in her ear.
The life went out of her,
but she was not scared.
You were tall and dark and your beauty
was your random acts of kindness.

In Memory of My Aunt Dorothy

I

What I miss most is the sound of your voice
and the way it reminded me, eerily,
of my mother's voice. After years
of not speaking I was beginning to know you,
not as the instrument that brought my father down,
but as a person who loved life
and saw no reason to apologize
for getting as much out of it as you could.
People loved you, and I loved you,
for the laughter in your voice,
the concern you showed for friends,
the wide range of your interests,
your willingness to tell your story,
and to give of yourself in the telling
without stint, with no strings attached.
There was something wonderful in that,
which now, with your death, is cut short.

II

You were ambitious like no one else in the family,
invariably well-dressed, in fine clothes and furs,
your eye fixed on symbols of status –
or what passed for status in our town.
Golf, tennis, and bridge allowed you entry
into the circles where you could rub shoulders
with people of like mind. You loved big words
and the cachet big words conferred.
You looked down on my father,
a mere plumber, a man of few words,
who did not have the gift of gab like you,
or the wit, and you had the power,
when you took ownership of his company,
to make his life miserable. Inwardly railing,
he fought to break free from your tyranny.
Are you to blame if he ultimately failed?

III

But because you loved words for the way
they opened doors, I was glad to stay
with you, when I was four and could not read,
and learn the difference between see and seed.

And because you wanted me to thrive,
I felt special in your company and more alive
than when I was left on my own, to roam
the neighborhood in search of a home.

And because you took me under your wing
and taught me that words too can sing,
I thought you were the source of magic
and not the root of what was tragic.

And because you helped me find
enduring value in things of the mind,
I remember you with affection,
in all your imperfection.

Are We Getting Anywhere?

In our marriage I find
moments of sharing, hurts
and forgivenesses, joys
that are greatest because
no one else knows them.
We promised not to hide
anything from each other
because any thought or feeling,
kept secret, is a wedge
that's certain to drive us apart.
The years have swept aside
such bravado, and we know
what we've always known –
that we are comforted
and reassured by the solitariness
each sees in the other.

The life of less fortunate creatures
was always important to you.
You feel a real sadness
for animals found dead by the road,
dogs chained in backyards and left
to bark and whine the live-long day,
chickens kept in boxes for slaughter,
all farm animals cruelly treated.
Sometimes the smallest hurt
sends you into a downward spiral
and I know you're re-living
an almost pre-historic wound.
Like Ulysses adrift at sea
I strap myself to the mast,
hoping to outlast the storm.

Trees were your best friends
when you were a child,
you once explained to me,
and I wonder if, in your mind,
I'm like one of those trees –
tall, straight, solitary, giving
little of myself, but always
present, ready to hold you,

and be held. Something binds
us close after all these years,
though we'd be hard pressed
to say exactly in what way
we are getting anywhere.

Opening the River
For Daniel LeBlanc

And for so long your heart
has been blocked, allowing
no passage of deep emotion.
Thoughts of your children,
those offspring, those fish
you had taken such pride in,
it was you who let them slip
and fade from memory.
Instead, you spent your time
building up your arguments
like silt in your sleek channels,
always higher, more convoluted,
mud banks with peaks and valleys
where you could wholly swallow
your most persistent adversaries.
They were good arguments, yes,
having to do with your view
of how we should live with nature,
working with her, not against her.
But they were arguments all the same,
which remained at a certain level
of dryness, and they did not have
the wetness of things heartfelt.
Because we admired you
and because we appreciated
your many sacrifices –
the time you gave to the cause,
the taunts you endured,
the ridicule you tried
to ignore but which clearly
wounded you deeply –
it was to you we looked,
as our leader and our keeper,
the day the gates were lifted.

Ah, what a moment that was!
Friend and foe alike watched
in awe as one by one the huge
metal slabs rose, unleashing
the swirl of waters held back

by the catastrophic causeway
this biblical stretch of time.
What joy you must have felt,
knowing you were whole again,
the salt of your ebbing and flowing
made one with the fresh calm
of your source. On the hillside
people called to friends and allies,
with shouts of congratulation,
encouragement, or consternation.
Overcome with emotion,
you wanted to throw yourself,
your whole body – your arms,
your face, your shoulders,
your rib cage, your belly,
your buttocks, your thighs –
into the churning waters if that
might have furthered the cause.

You flow more calmly now,
with a stateliness and assurance
you didn't have before.
Like a person rising up
from a fainting spell
or a near-death experience
you've taken on color –
blue with streaks of white.
And it's more than meets
the eye, because deep down,
where no one can see,
the fish are multiplying,
and they are hungry,
having been so long denied
entry into the silky confines
of your narrowing bed.

You have a dream
that one day you will wake
with joy in your heart,
knowing that you can take
the ups and downs,
the ebbs and flows
that life inevitably throws

your way, in stride,
with no fear of ever again
being cast away,
confined, or blocked
in anything you might desire
with sufficient desire.
And when that day comes
you will be free to be
what you were meant to be –
totally yourself.

Beckett and I

The man who answered the door was tall
and very thin, ghostly.
His face was quite youthful,
more beautiful even
than in the photos.
He said nothing
but received me in a very courtly way
and we sat at a very big, long table.
He poured me a glass of whiskey
and one for himself.
The room was clean, white, and bare.
He waited for me to talk.
I asked him about Joyce.
Did he compose songs?
He seemed relieved
to talk about Joyce
and not himself.
He sang one of Joyce's songs,
in a voice that was steady, flat,
and almost too soft to hear.
He asked me about myself.
Did I have any children?
I talked about my son's operation,
and he mentioned an article he'd read.
He had deep-set, blue eyes,
thick eyebrows, deeply furrowed
forehead, thick, wiry, whitish hair
cut short and brushed back.
It's time to go now, his silence said.
There was so much I wanted to tell him,
but I couldn't find the words.
I've never really wanted to meet
anyone else in my life, I wanted to say.
He ushered me to the door, said
nothing but bowed politely.
Though I'd stumbled, talked too much,
and not really said what I wanted to say,
what I felt, when cast out again,
was a reverence so deep
that nothing could touch it now.

Eros and Thanatos

After the meal, on the way home, in the quiet of the car,
With the music turned down low, what you'd like to think
About is how, in the spirit of fairness, to split the tab at the bar
In light of the fact, agreed to long ago, that you don't drink
As much as I do, not even half. What you fail to take
Into account, I'm quick to point out, is the piece of cake
You ordered at the end of the meal. You know I wanted
None of it. It always begins this way, quietly sprung,
With a question, a slip of the tongue,
And before we know it we are hunter and hunted.

The meal itself, at the Tide 'n Boar, was pleasant enough,
You and I, long married, and two new friends, one of whom
Has to fly home to England tomorrow, a tough
Decision, when their love has just begun to bloom.
You sat next to Michael, I sat next to Jill.
We drank wine, we talked, we had our fill.
When loss of ego engenders union with one's mate,
The destructive element in love works to the good,
But for some, more poorly understood,
Loss of ego and loss of self are easy to conflate.

Instead of splitting the bill evenly down the middle
You'd like me to pony up for the glass of wine,
And in this way, with something so trivial, you'd piddle
With an understanding we've painfully arrived at, a line
In the sand we've agreed it's best not to cross
For fear of putting everything at risk of loss.
My income is much less than yours, it's true,
I know what you spend on house, on car, on food
But I'm in no mood
To be hammered and lashed until I'm blue.

It's like a whip that you take out every week
Or two, to beat me with. I should take a room
Somewhere and live the life, subdued, meek,
I ought to be living, rather than stay in this tomb
We've dug for ourselves, with much mumbling,
Where everything must come tumbling
Down and all the love we've ever known
Amounts to nothing. All is subject to collapse

In the cold heat of relapse.
We must reap what we've sown.

At the top of the driveway a pheasant scurries
For cover, still unsure of us, though he's been around
Before, many times, still afraid we'll let loose the cold furies
Of our discontent. From the house next door comes the sound
Of laughter, and we can see a light in the window upstairs
Where the young couple, a boy and a girl, converse, with no cares
In the world save the care they show for each other.
Instead of going inside we wait awhile on the porch,
Let them become for us a torch
That leads us back, almost against our wills, to each other.

Fortitude of Obstacle

To undertake is to achieve
Be Undertaking blent
With fortitude of obstacle
And toward encouragement

                                  - Emily Dickinson

For example when you come down the stairs
One step at a time, hesitantly, as you face
Obstacles both old and new – such as failing
Eyesight, chronic weakness in the legs, poor
Memory, including for example how many steps
Are there to the bottom, or a memory that's too
Vivid, such as the memory of the pain that sometimes
Shoots through your hip – as you continue on down
What is there for me to do but watch and wait.

In the end it's not the money that counts, nor the prizes
You've won, but the people you love, and the people
Who love you. It's having work you wake up to
Every day with an intense desire to get at it.
It's not even happiness you seek or pursue,
At least not directly, but to be among people
You know you can trust and depend on. It's to know
You have survived, you did what you had to do
To survive in the face of whatever life could throw
Your way, in the shape of an obstacle, a hurdle,
A puzzle, or a trauma. Even more than wisdom,
Even more than happiness, even more than to be lucky
In your choice of friends, it is fortitude that matters.

But don't forget that although much has been lost
Much has also been gained, such as no longer living
Every moment thinking what your duty might be,
What you must do, without fail, before you can rest,
And also there's the sense that you no longer have to impress
Anybody for any reason, you are who you are and it's time
To stop feeling bad about yourself or thinking you must
Find excuses for this or that shortcoming.
And the really great thing is that you begin to bring
Your various cravings and addictions under control,

And you begin to feel a closing of the gap between
What the body demands and what the mind wants.

It's like when you enter a church and the candles
Are flickering and they begin to go out one by one,
And you wonder just how dark is it going to get,
And the surprise is that in the dark everything
Has its own shape and its own feel and everything
Is alive with its own energy and everything
Exists in the moment or not at all. The dark
Is no longer an obstacle but an opening
Into a space or realm in which
You have no memory of growing old.

Lament
For Irmi

I

I thought we would have something to say
to each other at the end, but apparently not.
This is a great sadness. You made no effort,
as far as I know, to call me or send word
that you were ill. What we experienced
together, the early years at university,
the joy of finding so much in common,
coming to a new country, children,
work, travel, the apartments we rented,
the houses we owned, the places we lived,
the hard times, the divorce, all this and more,
is there anyone but me who still cares
about any of this, now that you are gone?

The children were your greatest achievement.
Being a mother suited you well. For a while
it didn't seem possible, but it happened,
and you took full advantage and attained
a sort of perfection, growing far beyond
what you had been, answerable to no one,
in no one's shadow. You were everything
you were meant to be, caring, strict, tender,
sometimes short-tempered, always proud.
How sad then that you were caught up,
at the end, in a dispute between your son
and daughter, unable, except briefly
with your death, to bind the wounds.

Against all the voices, all the confusion
you struggled to be whole again.
But instead of reaching out to others
you turned inward. You told no one,
or very few. You did not want us to know.
You wanted to save yourself for the battle
ahead, but the battle was already lost.
Even now, a year after your death,
you continue to keep your distance,
refusing to enter into my dreams,

or take any part in my waking life.
None of my other dead have refused
to return to me as you have refused.

II

All your life you were good at endings.
Family, friends, lovers, when outgrown,
you left behind, like a snake sheds its skin
as it continues to grow, and also as a way
to rid itself of parasites. Why should I be
surprised that you had nothing to say
to me, during your illness, and in the days
and weeks after your death? Did you not
once stop to think I might have wanted
to talk with you and reach some sort
of understanding? I suppose you had your
reasons, but they remain as mysterious to me
today as they were when we were married.

Flowers, trees, shrubs, grass, various animals
that remain during the harsh winter months,
in hibernation, or protected by layers of fur
or thickly oiled feathers, all find a way
to survive, but you, you too easily gave up
the fight. You too readily chose alternative
therapies, eschewing the harsher but proven
remedies. What bad advice did your friends
give you, the few you confided in? The insiders
you cultivated, who thought like you and wrapped
themselves in the cloak of superior wisdom.
Why did you listen to them? I don't blame you,
I blame them. You could be here with us still.

You had no need to take anyone's advice.
You had a mind of your own, and a will
as close to unbreakable as any I've seen.
A decision, once made, was a path in the forest
from which there could be no turning back.
This served you well, in a life where the odds
were stacked against you. It had its dark side,
inevitably. A strong will, when thwarted,
lashes out in anger. The leaf that shines bright

in the sun has a dark underside where the slug
clings, and makes itself at home, and eats.
In everything, you had to come out on top.
With you it was either give way, or fight.

III

You continued to work almost to the end.
It is what you wanted, more than anything.
You loved your work, and you were widely
admired for the skill you brought to it,
and the kindness you showed to clients.
I'm glad you received the recognition
you deserved, even if it came from those
who did not know you, though they thought
they did. It was the middle of May when you
surprised us with your dying. The lilac bush
had hardly begun to bloom. The tulips, under
one last snowfall, had wilted. The crocuses
and the snow-drops had come and gone.

For a long time you kept even the children
in the dark. What were you thinking?
What if you had died even more quickly
than you did, before you had called them home?
What a catastrophe that would have been.
But in the end, as if by some miracle, both
your daughter and your son were at your side.
What more can you ask, than to be surrounded
at the end of life by those you most love?
Though I was not there, and my experience
of the event amounts to less than nothing,
I find solace in the knowledge that they
were with you, and they remember it.

The range of your interests and talents
was remarkable. Widely traveled, fluent
in five languages, a published researcher,
a popular teacher, you continued to seek
new ways of living and working that better
reflected who you were. As you gained
confidence, the outlines of your character

became clear. Whatever brought you closer
to completion as a human being you embraced.
Whatever did not, you let go. You learned
to listen. As others opened themselves to you,
you opened yourself to the larger world.
All that was creative in you flowered.

Café Joe Moka

All the tables in the court area were taken,
except one, which I claimed. You sat down
next to me for the very good reason
that there was no other place to sit.
I was alone, new to town, and I had yet
to talk to anyone, other than the man
behind the bar at Boomerangs. When
I told you I was in town to open a bookstore,
your interest was immediately sparked.
We talked about books, about films,
about art galleries, about good places to eat,
about nature trails and bird sanctuaries.
You mentioned the Sackville Film Society
and you said you could drive me to the next
showing if I didn't have a car, which seemed
overly generous given that you barely
knew me. You said you liked the shirt
I was wearing, a pink, long-sleeved shirt
though it was mid-summer. I told you where
I planned to locate my store, and you
said you'd come by some day. You pointed
in the general direction of where you lived
and said you had to be going. I didn't see
you for several weeks and almost gave up
hope I'd ever see you again. You'd been away,
you explained, at a family reunion. We talked,
and it was like picking up a thread we'd left
hanging just the day before. You kept coming
into the bookstore, you said, because you liked
being in my company. What I liked was
your smile, the sound of your voice,
and the fact that you genuinely
wanted to hear what I had to say.

ACKNOWLEDGMENTS

Thanks to *The Antigonish Review* where five of these poems first
appeared, including "To My Brother, On His Serenely Facing Death,"
"Something Happened," "Overheard," "Beckett and I," and "Lament."
"My Father, My Enemy, and My Father" was included in the anthology
Crossing Lines: Poets Who Came to Canada in the Vietnam War Era
(Seraphim Editions, 2008).
Line 5 of "My Father, My Enemy, and My Father" is taken from Dylan
Thomas.
"The Legacy" is based on a poem written by my sister, Judy Lemond,
for a creative writing class.
"Fed Up" has close parallels with a poem called "Walking Around"
by Pablo Neruda.
Certain lines in the poem "On the Anniversary of My Mother's Death"
are drawn from a letter from my friend Robert Bubrovszky of Paris, France.
"The Necessity of Belief" owes its diction and some of its imagery
to the journals of Krishnamurti.
"If You Are Waiting for Anything" grew out of a workshop that Robert
Bly gave in Moncton at the Northrop Frye Literary Festival in April, 2001.
"Barrington Street, Halifax" is better than it was because of Wesley McNair.
"Something Happened" is for my daughter Anna.
"Love Poem to My Brother" is for my brother Bob.

ABOUT THE AUTHOR

Edward Lemond has lived in the Moncton, New Brunswick area since 1993.
Before that he lived for 24 years in Halifax, Nova Scotia. He grew up in
Long Beach, California and Lafayette, Indiana, and came to Canada in 1969.
He is a former bookseller and one of the founders of the Northrop Frye
Literary Festival, held annually in Moncton, Frye's home town.

His novel, *The Baptism of Alden Oakes,* won first prize in the novel category
at the 1986 Writers' Federation of Nova Scotia competition. His novella, *Birds of
Appetite,* was short-listed for the 2011 Ken Klonsky Novella Contest, sponsored by
Quattro Books. His novel, *Equal Affection,* won second place in the 2013 competition for
the Richards Prize, sponsored by the Writers' Federation of New Brunswick.

www.ingramcontent.com/pod-product-compliance
Lightning Source LLC
Chambersburg PA
CBHW031323040426
42443CB00005B/204